MARTIAL ARTS

Kendo

'Highly recommended reading for any aspiring martial artist. This series will enhance your knowledge of styles, history, grading systems and finding and analyzing the right club.'

Stan 'The Man' Longinidis
8-times World Kickboxing
Champion

PAUL COLLINS

This edition first published in 2002 in the United States of America by Chelsea House Publishers, a subsidiary of Haights Cross Communications.

Chelsea House Publishers
1974 Sproul Road, Suite 400
Broomall, PA 19008-0914

The Chelsea House world wide web address is www.chelseahouse.com

Library of Congress Cataloging-in-Publication Data Applied for.

ISBN 0-7910-6869-2

First published in 2002 by
MACMILLAN EDUCATION AUSTRALIA PTY LTD
627 Chapel Street, South Yarra, Australia 3141

Copyright © Paul Collins 2002

Text design and page layout by Judith Summerfeldt Grace
  and Jacinta Hanrahan
Cover design by Judith Summerfeldt Grace
Edited by Carmel Heron

Printed in China

Acknowledgments
The author would like to thank Mr. Nagae and his instructors from the Melbourne Budokai, Kensikan Dojo, Australia for the use of his dojo when taking the photographs in this book.

Photographs by Nick Sandalis except p. 9 © Geostock and p. 11 courtesy of Consulate-General of Japan, Melbourne.

**Techniques used in this book should only be practiced
under qualified supervision.**

Contents

What are martial arts?

Most people have seen at least one fantastic martial arts movie. A lot of it is trick photography. A **ninja** cannot really jump backwards and land on the roof of a towering house! Then again, martial arts are about belief—belief in yourself and your ability to overcome any obstacle, no matter how big or small.

Ask any martial arts student why they train and the answer will be to learn **self-defense**. But that answer only scratches the surface of the term 'martial arts'.

One of the many functions of martial arts is to train students, both physically and mentally.

Martial arts have ancient traditions steeped in discipline and dedication. Most martial arts have developed from ancient Asian combat skills. In **feudal** times, people in Asia had to defend themselves against attack. Quite often, peasants were not allowed to carry weapons, so self-defense became their weapon.

Some martial arts are fighting sports, such as karate and kung fu. Other martial arts, like tai chi, concentrate on self-improvement, although self-defense is part of the training.

Ninjutsu

Kung fu

Karate

The word 'martial' comes
from Mars, the Roman
god of war.

Dedication and discipline

Kendo is hard work. Ask any senior student. Dedication plays a
major role in the life of a martial arts enthusiast. Training can be
up to four times a week and an average session lasts from 60 to
90 minutes.

Students practice one simple
procedure over and over again.
They might repeat a move
200 times in one training
session, only to repeat the
same move the next time
they train. Martial artists
learn through repetition,
so that even the most
basic moves can be
automatically performed
when they are suddenly
required.

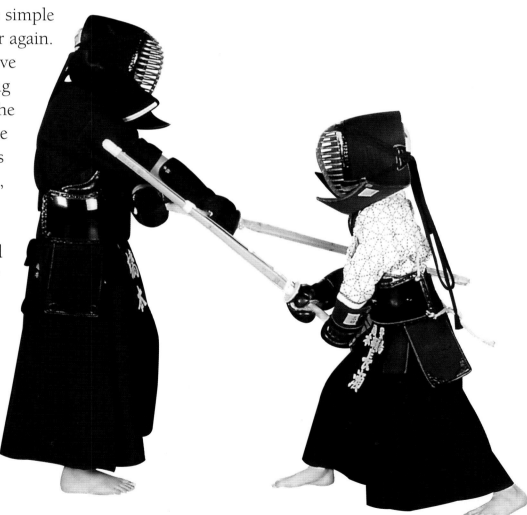

Kendo

Understanding kendo

Kendo is the Japanese art of two-handed fencing. 'Ken' translated means 'sword', and 'do' means 'way' or 'path'. Kendo is based solely on swordfighting—there are no grappling techniques, kicks or punches.

The art of kendo originated in Japan where it was first practiced by the **samurai**. For this reason, kendo is more popular in Japan than anywhere else in the world.

Kendo is based solely on swordfighting.

Being a student of kendo involves learning more than just swordfighting, however. For students of kendo, called *kendoka*, self-improvement is very important. Kendo promotes benefits such as:

⊙ inner peace and calm

⊙ self-control and well being

⊙ precision and speed

⊙ self-discipline and confidence.

There are many reasons why people practice kendo. Some want to master the art, while others practice it for exercise, as a sport, and to learn swordsmanship.

Kendo is the Japanese art of two-handed fencing.

Kendo should not be seen as sport but as a lifetime's study.

Anonymous

Japan: the birthplace of kendo

Population:	126.2 million
Language:	Japanese
Currency:	Yen (¥)
Main religions:	Shinto, Buddhism and Christianity

Japan leads the world as a fishing nation. This is because it is a nation of mountainous islands in the North Pacific Ocean. The four main islands are Honshu, Kyushu, Shikoku and Hokkaido. They are situated off the mainland of east Asia. Tokyo, on the island of Honshu, is the capital city of Japan.

Many of Japan's mountains are active volcanoes, which often cause earthquakes. Mount Fuji is Japan's tallest mountain. It is 3,776 meters (12,390 feet) high and it is an extinct volcano.

The government of Japan is a democratic government, elected by the people. The head of government is the Prime Minister. The Emperor of Japan is the ceremonial head of state.

Kyushu

Shikoku

Pacific Ocean

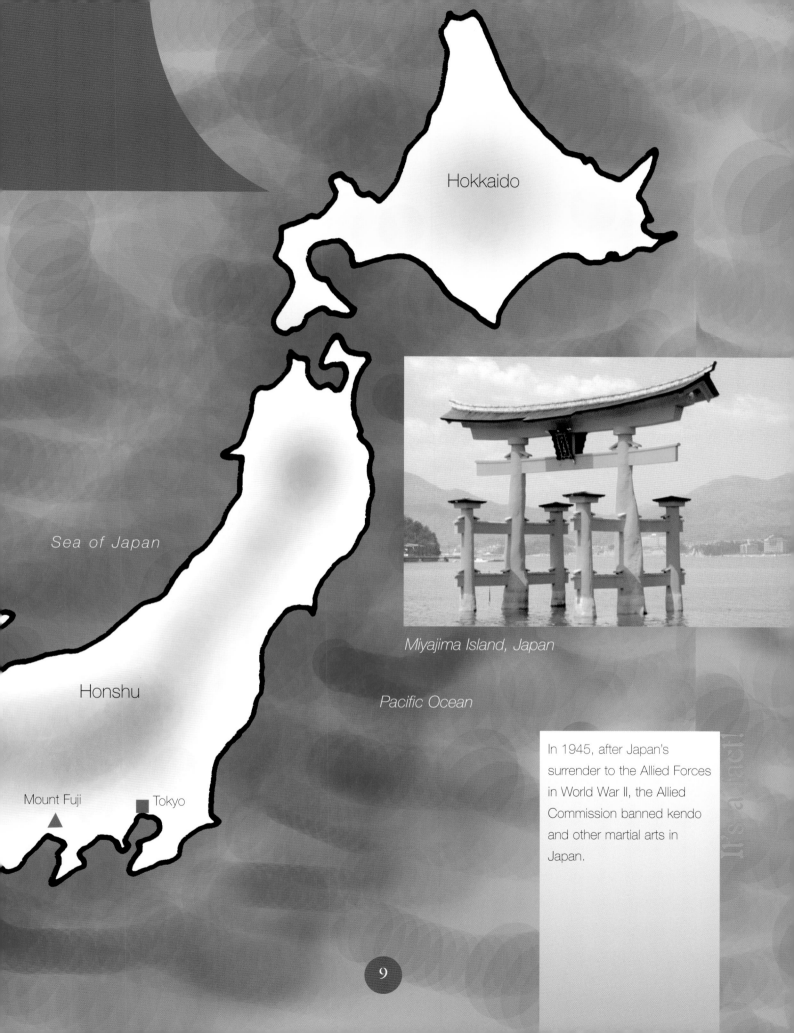

Hokkaido

Sea of Japan

Honshu

Mount Fuji ▲   ■ Tokyo

Miyajima Island, Japan

Pacific Ocean

In 1945, after Japan's surrender to the Allied Forces in World War II, the Allied Commission banned kendo and other martial arts in Japan.

It's a fact!

The history of kendo

Modern-day kendo originated from kenjutsu, a Chinese swordfighting art practiced more than 1500 years ago.

In Japan, kenjutsu was practiced by the samurai, the warrior class of Japan. In ancient times, real swords and training used to be so dangerous that students and instructors were often killed. Because of this, armor was introduced in the 1600s to provide some protection. In the 1700s, the *shinai* (bamboo stick) was introduced in practice. A replica of the sword, called a *bokuto* (made from wood), was used to practice **kata**. The *shinai* and *bogu* made training much safer and injuries were reduced.

During the Tokugawa period (1600–1750), kenjutsu became a much less violent art. After many years of continuous war, Japan became a peaceful country. Kenjutsu was practiced as an art form but not used in violence.

In 1912, kenjutsu masters from different clubs came together to officially develop a new system of kenjutsu. This new system was called kendo to mark the difference in style. The aim of kenjutsu was to defeat the opponent, whereas the aim of kendo is more to do with self-development and improvement.

It's a fact!

A law was passed in 1907 that made learning kendo compulsory in all Japanese schools.

Prior to World War II, it was compulsory for all Japanese boys to learn kendo. After Japan's defeat in the war, kendo was banned because of its warlike tradition. By 1952, a less aggressive version of kendo was introduced into Japan. Today, kendo is as popular in Japan as football is in America.

The first college of the Kendo Federation was opened in 1913. Today, in Japan alone, more than three million students practice kendo.

Kendo is as popular in Japan as football is in America.

Dress code and etiquette

Head cloth worn under the *men* (tenugui)

Head guard (men)

Chest and side protectors (do)

Gloves (kote)

Lower body protector (tare)

Bamboo sword (shinai)

The full dress of a kendoka *showing the armor worn over the* kendogi

Dress code

On the battlefield, swordsmen wore armor. The style of armor worn has changed over the years, but it still protects the people who practice kendo.

Before training, a ritual is performed where *kendoka* neatly lay out their uniforms and put on their face guards and gloves.

The entire uniform, called a *kendogi*, includes a woven cotton top (*keikogi*) and pleated skirt-like pants that are called *hakama*. The armor is worn over the *kendogi* and is made up of four pieces:

⊚ a head guard (*men*), which has a metal face grill and protective flaps covering the throat and the back of the head and shoulders

⊚ a body protector (*do*), which is made from bamboo and covered in leather

⊚ gloves (*kote*), which are thickly padded and protect the wrists

⊚ a hip and waist protector (*tare*), which is a thick cotton belt with protective flaps hanging from it.

For protection, the most important part of a *kendoka's* uniform is the head guard. A special towel (*tenugui*) is placed around the head before putting on the head guard. *Kendoka* also wear groin protectors.

Etiquette

Kendo schools require students to show proper respect for their *sensei* (instructor), fellow students and *dojo* (training hall).

◉ Always bow when entering the *dojo*. It is a sign of respect to your *sensei* and to the past and present masters of kendo. Always bow to your *sensei* when asking for or receiving instruction.

◉ Touching another student's gear, such as their armor or their sword, is not allowed unless you have permission to do so. Always pass behind a *kendoka* wearing armor. If passing in front of a seated *kendoka*, pause, give a slight bow and hold out your hand as you pass.

◉ Uniforms must be kept clean and in good order at all times.

◉ Students must respect their *shinai*. Although it is made from bamboo, it represents a fighter's sword, and this was extremely important to any swordsman. A kendoka should never lean on their *shinai*, or leave it lying around. It would be considered disrespectful to step over another student's armor or weapons that are laid out on the floor.

◉ When adjusting your uniform, you must move to the side of the *dojo* and kneel before readjusting it. It is a sign of disrespect to reposition any part of your armor while standing. This ritual originates from the battlefield where samurai warriors were vulnerable if caught standing up to readjust their armor.

◉ Be punctual. This is a sign of discipline, dedication and respect.

◉ Remove footwear before entering the *dojo*. The Japanese do not usually wear outdoor shoes inside.

◉ Smoking, drinking and eating are not tolerated in the *dojo*.

◉ If *yame* is called, it means stop what you are doing immediately.

Bowing is the most common way of showing respect for instructors and fellow students.

Bowing to chief instructor

Class bows to chief instructor

Did you know?

Bowing is another form of shaking hands. It stems from Japanese feudal times when people bowed to show that they trusted the other person not to lop off their head with a sword. In the west, people shake hands, which initially proved that they did not carry a weapon in their right hand. This was a sign of good faith.

Before you start

Choosing a club

A look through the telephone book under the general heading 'Martial Arts' will show you where the nearest clubs are.

It is better to join a large club with many members. Also ensure that the club has students about your own age. If not, you could always join with a friend.

If money is a consideration, phone around and compare costs. Some clubs charge a joining fee, while other clubs only charge per visit. Visitors normally do not pay, so it is a good idea to sit in on a session or two before joining a club.

Joining a martial arts club can be fun. Club members can sign up for competitions and travel interstate or even overseas to represent their club. Some clubs also organize weekend camps.

Clothing and equipment

Kendo is perhaps the most expensive martial art to study. The armor is costly to purchase and younger students soon grow out of it. However, your first few training sessions can be performed in a pair of loose pants and a T-shirt.

Clubs should have all the protective equipment you will need, like leg and arm guards, although it is better to buy your own once you start to train seriously. Personal equipment can be kept in better condition and will fit better than the standard club equipment. Second-hand padded guards and even gloves can be bought at recycled equipment stores and through personal advertisements in newspapers. Garage sales are also a good source of second-hand martial arts equipment.

You could even ask the club that you are joining if any older students have uniforms that are now too small for them. This will also save you from having to buy the club's badges and sew them on.

wakizashi

katana

bokuto (short)

bokuto (long)

shinai

The swords used in kendo

Insurance

Insurance is advised, although you are unlikely to get badly injured at a well-run martial arts school. Most clubs have insurance coverage so it pays to ask.

Confidence and disabilities

Everyone feels nervous when they first enter a club. Once you have met some fellow students you will feel a lot more confident.

A light stretching workout before training is a good way to relax and to loosen stiff muscles. Good instructors will teach you breathing techniques, which will calm you and help you to focus.

A disability should not stop you from trying kendo. Many top athletes have **asthma**. Other athletes have **diabetes**. Getting fit through kendo can help improve your overall condition. Just make sure your instructor knows of your complaint, take necessary precautions and bow out when you do not feel well.

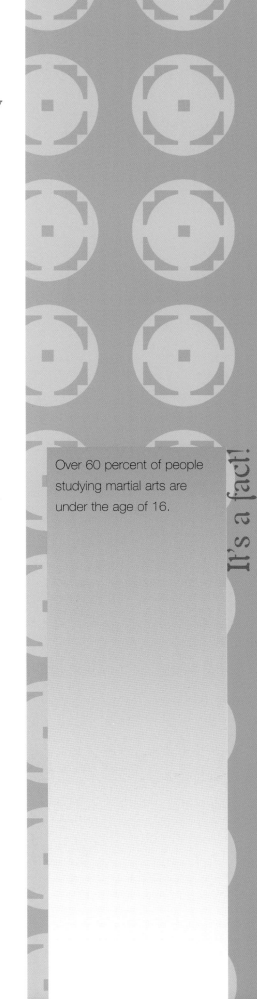

Over 60 percent of people studying martial arts are under the age of 16.

It's a fact!

17

Fitness and training

Beginner martial artists are not usually ready for serious training. This takes time. They need to build fitness slowly. Most martial arts clubs have a beginners' class, where students learn the basics of their sport and get fit.

At the start of each training session, students perform warm-up and stretching exercises. Some clubs do aerobic exercises for fitness. The instructor will then teach the class something new or ask the class to practice a technique with partners. Partner training teaches timing, reaction, balance, self-control and countering skills.

*Cleaning the floor is performed before every training session. This is done for **hygiene** reasons and to avoid injury. One of the responsibilities of members of the kendo community is to keep everything in good order for the benefit of others.*

Hitting the drum starts and stops training. One strike commences training, and two strikes stop it. Five strikes mean the end of the training session. Beating the drum can also be used to count time when students perform certain techniques.

Stretching

As well as fitness you will need to gain flexibility and greater mobility. This means stretching all your body parts. You need to loosen and warm tight and cold muscles.

It is important to keep each stretching movement gentle and slow. You should not use jerking or bouncing movements.

Stretching has many purposes. It:

- increases heart and lung capacity

- helps you practice movements you are about to perform

- helps avoid injury from pulled muscles

- gives you greater flexibility.

It is equally important to cool down after exercising. This maintains the level of blood circulation and reduces muscle spasms. Gentle cool-down stretches also help prevent injuries, because they reduce muscle tightness.

Limbering wrists

Warming shoulders

Stretching calves and legs

Warming laterals

Sparring

Kendo is a full-contact sport, so students must learn how to take a hit as well as how to deliver one. *Jigeiko* is the term used for sparring—when you practice what you have learned with a partner. Students can develop their techniques against opponents to see what works for them and what does not. When sparring, a student does not know which techniques their partner is going to use, and timing and precision become very important.

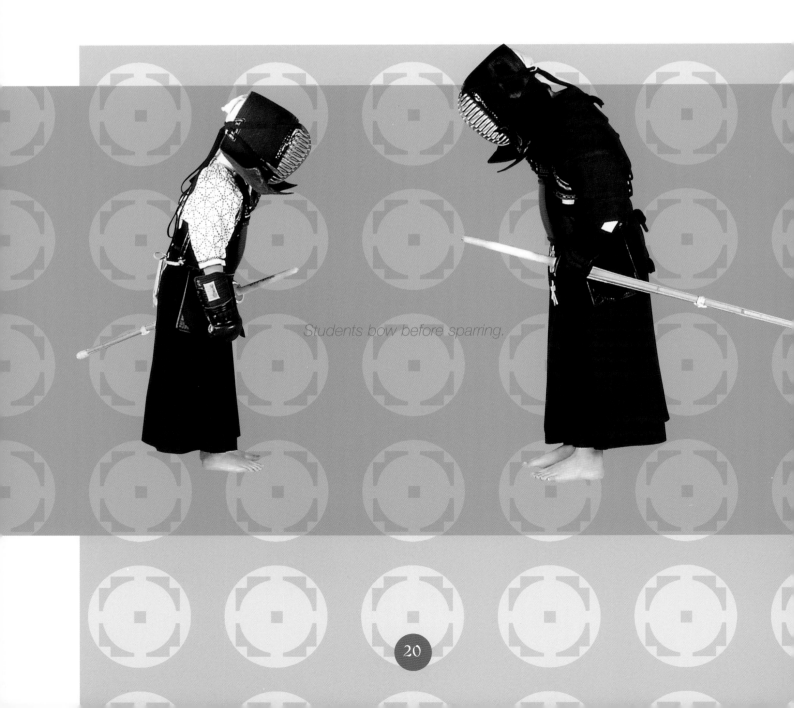

Students bow before sparring.

Jigeiko is not competitive as there is no winner or loser. It is a method of practicing so that students learn from one another. The rules of *jigeiko* are set by the instructor.

Before students commence sparring, they warm up by running around the *dojo*. They also practice simple techniques up and down the *dojo*. One partner will attack and the other will defend, then they switch so the defender becomes the attacker. This warm-up exercise is always performed with *shinai*.

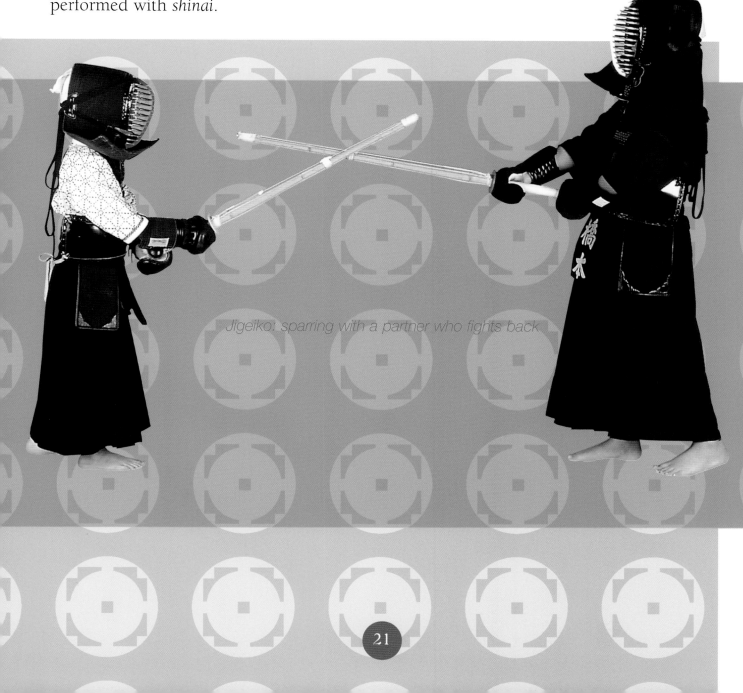

Jigeiko: sparring with a partner who fights back

Kendo techniques

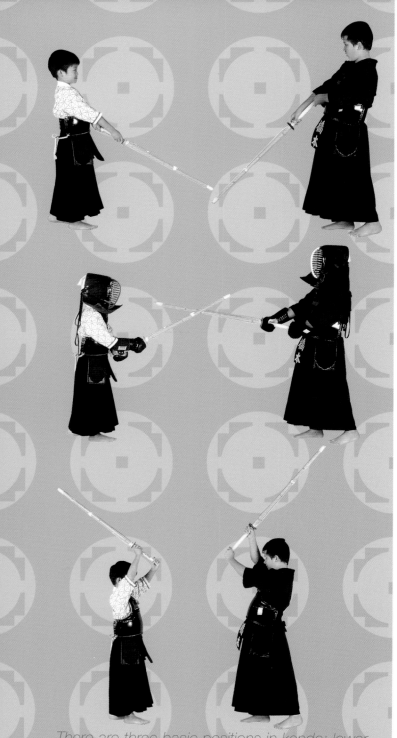

There are three main body parts that *kendoka* try to strike. These are:

- the forearm (*kote*), also known as the lower position
- either side of the body (*do*), also known as the middle position
- the top or either side of the head (*men*), also known as the high position.

It is from these three positions that students earn the most points in competition.

Nowadays these body parts are protected by armor, but they were much more vulnerable in the days of the samurai.

In kendo, a good overall technique involves the combination of correct posture, footwork and striking techniques.

A good, strong posture is important in kendo. If you are slightly unbalanced, you will deliver an ineffective strike and you can be easily caught unguarded by your opponent.

There are three basic positions in kendo: lower (gedan-no-kame), middle (jodan-no-kamae) and high (chudan-no-kamae) positions.

In a standing position your feet should be shoulder-width apart. Students keep their back heels slightly raised in preparation for retreat or attack. Movement can be made in eight directions: forwards, backwards, left, right and any diagonal. Students must keep their upright postures while practicing, so that they are prepared for offensive and defensive movements.

Good technique also includes holding your weapon correctly. A firm grip is important for both strength in striking and keeping a hold of your sword.

Head strike

Forearm strike

Holding your weapon correctly is important for good technique.

Practicing on a dummy perfects technique.

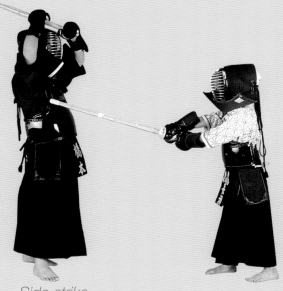

Side strike

Training in armor is often referred to as jigeiko. Contact is made on the score areas that are protected by the armor. It is here that kata work pays off!

Kata (forms)

Like most martial arts, kendo has *kata*. *Kata* are a series of movements which students practice over and over again. *Kata* enable students to practice moves they have learned, with or without a partner. *Kata* are performed with *bokuto* and without armor, and blows are not allowed to touch a partner's body.

There are ten *kata*. Techniques in each *kata* are designed to practice defensive and attacking moves. Seven *kata* are demonstrations of techniques using the long sword, and three *kata* are demonstrations of techniques using the short sword against the long sword. The techniques learned by beginners are demonstrated in the first *kata*. The attacker is called the *uchitachi* and the defender is called the *shidachi*.

Suburi

Kendoka also practice *suburi*, which are basic 'cutting' techniques performed while continuously moving backwards and forwards. Students do not 'hack and slash' with their swords. They learn to strike their opponents in a perfected manner.

Suburi are performed without armor and are designed to develop focus, stamina and technique. As each cutting movement is performed, *kendoka* shout. This is called a *kakegoe*. *Kakegoe* is a shout that releases energy for power and helps a *kendoka* to focus.

Basic moves and posture in kendo

These are some of the most common moves that you will learn in kendo.

Ashi gamae: correct positioning of the feet is important, so that a student can respond to their opponent's attack or retreat immediately.

Chudan no kamae: this is the most common **stance** in kendo. The student holds the **hilt** of their sword a fist's length from their belly button, with the tip of the sword pointed at their opponent's throat.

Fumi komi ashi: a student kicks off with their left foot to shorten the distance between them and their opponent. This is usually just one large step forward.

Gedan no kamae: in this defensive stance, a student directs the tip of their sword at their opponent's kneecap.

Issoku itto no maai: this is a strategy concerning distance. It is considered that about 180 centimeters (6 feet) is the best distance between retreat and attack. You can attack with one large step forward and retreat with one large step back.

Kakari-geiko: a junior student practices with all their might, using all of the kendo skills they have learned without worrying about being attacked. Students usually perform *kakari-geiko* for a short time, or as long as their energy lasts.

Correct moves and posture come in handy during jigeiko.

Ken-sen: this is the tip of the sword or *shinai*. It is important to keep the *ken-sen* at the center of the opponent and be alert to opportunities of both attack and retreat.

Kiri-kaeshi: students learn to strike the *men* dead center and to both left and right sides.

Mawari-geiko: all the students of the club form two lines facing one another. They rotate continuously so that everyone faces a different opponent after every few minutes of fighting. It is extremely exhausting!

Suri-ashi: this is the technique of dragging your soles across the floor. This method helps steady the lower body, which allows the upper body to move freely.

Tai-atari: students learn how to collide with extra force with an opponent. The purpose of this is to upset the opponent's balance, thereby making them vulnerable to a strike.

The language of kendo

Most commands you hear in kendo are spoken in Japanese. It is a sign of respect to know Japanese. A *kendoka* can travel anywhere in the world and understand the language of kendo.

Japanese words sound the way they are written. For instance, *sensei* is pronounced 'sen-say'. 'G' is pronounced like the 'g' in 'get', not like the 'g' in 'gentle'. 'I' is pronounced 'ee'.

To learn kendo, you will need to know some of the following expressions. Some of the terms can vary from club to club.

chudan	basic position
datotsu	strike or point (in competition)
dojo	training hall
hajime	start
kakegoe	a shout to produce more power and energy when striking
keiko	free practice, sparring without set patterns
kendogu	armor
kendoka	a student of kendo
mokuso	**meditation**

rei	a bow	
sensei	instructor	
shiai	competition	
shinai	fiberglass or four-piece bamboo sword used for practice and competition	
suburi	basic sword swinging techniques	
yame	stop	
zanshin	determined or unshakable spirit, even after striking, in case of counter attack. In addition to this, if you use all of your strength in a strike, your energy will rejuvenate	

Counting one to ten

ichi	one	1
ni	two	2
san	three	3
shi	four	4
go	five	5
roku	six	6
shichi	seven	7
hachi	eight	8
ku	nine	9
ju	ten	10

It's a fact!

In Japanese, the singular and plural forms of a word are often the same. For instance, the plural of *dojo* is *dojo* and the plural of *kendoka* is still *kendoka*.

29

Competition

It is very important for *kendoka* to compete. It is only by competing with other students that *kendoka* can tell if their techniques are good or bad. Judges look for many qualities in competitors. These include composure, good posture and strong strikes against opponents. A good strike is delivered with confidence.

Students are always reminded to remain calm. Violent attacking behavior, where the aim is simply to win, is frowned upon. It is considered good form to accept defeat, which will teach students how to improve for the future.

Championships are held in halls. The match area is a rectangle or square of 9 to 11 meters (29 to 36 feet) on each side. An 'X' is marked in the center of the court. Competition is called *shiai*. There are three referees on court. Competing *kendoka* are tagged with either a red or a white flag. When the judge holds up the colored flag that you have been tagged with, you have just scored a point!

A *shiai* lasts for about five minutes. The winner is the first to score two points—or a single point if time runs out. You score points by striking certain parts of the body: the head, the throat and the sides of the body.

In true sportsmanship, opponents call out where they intend to hit. So a student will call out *men* if they are aiming for the head, or *do* to either side of the breastplate, etc.

Team events and *kata* competitions are also held. Many clubs have their own tournaments, while some stage inter-club competitions.

There are many trophies to be won in kendo!

Competing kendoka are tagged with either a red or white flag. When the judge holds up your colored flag, you have just scored a point!

Glossary

asthma	a breathing disorder	meditation	deep and serious thinking
Buddhism	a religion that started in Asia	ninja	traditionally a spy or assassin
diabetes	a disease where the body does not fully process sugar	samurai	Japanese warriors of ancient Japan
feudal	dating back to the Middle Ages, when all the land was owned by the nobility and the peasants worked for them	self-defense	usually grappling, which involves pinning your opponent so that they cannot strike you
		Shinto	a Japanese religion that worships ancestors
hilt	hand grip of a sword		
hygiene	cleanliness	stance	position
kata	forms or patterns of moves developed to improve technique by repetition		

Index